LIST YOUR CREATIVE SELF

Other Books by Ilene Segalove and Paul Bob Velick

List Your Self

List Your Self for Parents
(with Gareth Esersky)

Other Books by Ilene Segalove

Unwritten Letters

List Your Self for Pregnancy
(with Gareth Esersky)

List Your Self for Kids
(with Charlotte Blumenfeld)

LIST YOUR CREATIVE SELF

Listmaking as the Way
to Unleash Your Creativity

ILENE SEGALOVE AND PAUL BOB VELICK

Andrews McMeel
Publishing

Kansas City

*T*he LIST YOUR SELF book
series and calendars are the creation of
Ilene Segalove and Paul Bob Velick.
These listmaking tools invite the
reader to become the writer, offering an
interactive approach to self-discovery.

www.andrewsmcmeel.com

ISBN: 0-7407-0208-4

99 00 01 02 03 RDH 10 9 8 7 6 5 4 3 2 1

Book design by Holly Camerlinck
Illustrations by Nicholas Wilton

——— ATTENTION: SCHOOLS AND BUSINESSES ———

Andrews McMeel books are available at quantity discounts with bulk purchase for
educational, business, or sales promotional use. For information, please write to: Special Sales
Department, Andrews McMeel Publishing, 4520 Main Street, Kansas City, Missouri 64111.

CONTENTS

I dedicate this book to all the people who applauded whenever I did anything backward, crooked, or inside out. The list is long and surprising. And of course, to my parents, who thought everything I touched or altered was an inspired work of art, even when it wasn't.

—I.S.

I dedicate this creative journal to all those characters who have widened my path and yet still remain seen, heard, felt, known, and never forgotten. And to the soup that makes all things in this life possible, probable, and utterly fantastic: who woulda thunk.

—Paul Bob

INTRODUCTION

So what is creativity anyway? Is it a better idea, a quick right turn, an impulse that sprouts wings? Or is it simply turning nothing into something? Maybe it's walking backward, dying the dog orange, or serving seaweed and bananas on celery stalks at your next garden party. It's one of those words that defies definition. And that's very . . . creative. Creativity comes in all sizes, shapes, and colors. It's a big part of being human, just like the ability to reason, intuit, and wink. It's a natural impulse and a strong spark that lives inside each of us just waiting to ignite.

Creativity defies a simple explanation. It is a ball of contradiction and surprise. It takes form as both a focused genius solving a complicated problem and a raging goofball pulling ideas out of thin air. It's an innate talent and a calling we all share, yet much of the time it lurks, silent and invisible, just out of reach.

List Your Creative Self gives you the green light to enter the zone where your creativity lives and encourages you to explore. Through the pages you'll find a rich collection of one hundred list questions aimed at inspiring, releasing, and expanding your creative powers simply by listing whatever comes to mind. Creativity loves freedom, fun, and permission to flourish. *List Your Creative Self* is filled with a wide array of list questions that allow you to imagine, consider the alternatives, and dream away. It encourages you to make new discoveries about yourself and everyday life.

When does creativity strike? Consider these clues. Sometimes you may find yourself swapping words around in your mind and instantly whip up a new phrase, maybe kinda nonsensical but also far more profound and true than the original. What just happened? Are you losing it? Or might you actually be engaged in something far more exciting? Simply twisting up the status quo opens up a whole new world, a world that smacks of creativity.

Becoming a creative person is really a matter of changing your perspective and allowing yourself to embrace the unknown in life. Instead of squelching impulses, as creative urges percolate to the surface, let 'em fly. When you give yourself the freedom and permission to fan the inner spark, you'll be amazed at what's possible.

How did pretechnical man ever figure out that rubbing two sticks and a little moss would ignite into fire? Who discovered that smashing berries into liquid would make beautiful colors for painting, as well as great sparkling wines for drinking? Somebody probably asked a few potent questions to unleash the vital creative potential, and the answers flowed.

List Your Creative Self carries on the tradition by asking you to list all the creative tendencies you have, once had, or never had. It is a safe harbor where you can poke around, fine-tune, and tweak your creative impulses. For example, consider "List the ways you creatively solve everyday dilemmas and situations." At first you might think you don't have a creative bone in your body; you come up with only one answer:

- ✗ I ask everyone around me a lot of probing questions.

As you list, you might feel somewhat uncomfortable, raw, or even exposed. You might feel a little embarrassed. You may wonder if you are doing this right. Suspend all judgment. Your way is the right way. So you continue your listing:

- ✗ I do things backward
- ✗ I close my eyes and pretend I'm at the beach and then an answer floats my way
- ✗ I eat a piece of chocolate and relax
- ✗ I don't worry or panic
- ✗ I pretend I am an expert
- ✗ I laugh a lot

Original responses mean creative responses. Enjoy the feeling. And if it feels good you're right on track. Creating is playing, pure and simple. The play may turn into a project, a piece of art, an object of some sort, or not. It's important to remember the natural impulses of childhood that propelled you rather easily through the sandbox, the schoolyard, and even to the principal's office. To get warmed up, think about the following list question. Delve back into your memory if you need to.

List what you like to do when you "play."

- ✗ Walk for miles in the sun by the ocean along a path that is new to me
- ✗ Make something out of nothing for hours on end
- ✗ Listen to music and light a candle and close my eyes and take off on some wild journey in my mind

- Run in and out of as many art galleries as I can find
- Get lost
- Get a bunch of people together and have a feast
- Talk about things I know nothing about

List Your Creative Self is like having your very own day spa and personal creative coach in the palm of your hand. It is an easy and engaging tool that helps you discover your own creative style as well as being a great place to maintain and build new creative muscles.

Consider another list, perhaps something more imaginative. Remember, anything goes. "List how you would reorganize Main Street of your town if you were given free rein to do so."

- Reroute the cars elsewhere and plant trees, tropical plants, and orchids
- Paint the whole thing a bright green and decorate all the buildings with tiny mirrors
- Install a mini-newsstand with European magazines, big picture books, and poetry books
- Have plenty of chairs, and a large fountain filled with toy sail boats
- Great outdoor cafés, and paths for strolling
- Live classical music and jazz on weekends
- A big jungle, no people, no cars—we just have to stay on the outside and watch nature unfold

Creativity is not exclusive to special people; it's not limited to artists, writers, dancers, musicians, and poets. You don't need a license, a foreign accent, or a degree in higher learning. Creativity is not elitist nor does it demand a special outfit or lifestyle. It is not restricted to art studios, dance halls, science labs, and orchestra pits.

Creativity lives in our own kitchens as we conjure up new pancake recipes, in the backyard as we plant a new rose bush, and in our closets as we put together our Saturday-night outfits. It shows up in the way we solve problems, organize our desks, repair a faucet, and wax the car. It's a combination of the ingenuity, resourcefulness, and fun given to us at birth.

Every time we simply allow our original selves to be present, or come through whatever we are doing, we have expressed our own true creative identity. It may sound a bit overwhelming. What are our "true" original selves? Often it's the first answer out of our mouths, before we have time to censor and shut down. It's a set of personal preferences and particularities that some call eccentric.

When we are creating, time stands still and it is in that space of thought and action that we get to express our truest self. *List Your Creative Self* is the key to unlocking this creative process. Simply by filling in the one hundred provocative and probing list questions you'll discover a whole new world. The point is, accessing and engaging your true creative identity isn't that difficult. It's just a new process to learn and enjoy.

Creativity is a deep reservoir of infinite possibility just waiting to be called on, for any and all occasions. It pours out in the form of nonstop "what-ifs," sideways ideas, notions, realizations, discoveries, and instant methods that get us through the moments, minutes, hours, days, weeks, months, and years of life. So many well-known people have dedicated their lives to being creative. Many of them have influenced how you see yourself and the world. Consider the following list question:

List all the creative people, including sports stars, politicians, and scientists whom you admire.

- Vincent van Gogh
- Woody Allen
- Igor Stravinsky
- Jean Dubuffet
- Neil Diamond
- Henri Tolouse-Lautrec
- Stanley Kubrick
- Madonna
- John Cage
- Rudolph Nureyev
- Michael Jordan

It seems like these people just naturally took to being creative. This may or may not be so, but most of them pushed their own personal expression in spite of any self-doubt or setbacks. Some of us were told fairly early in life things like "You can't do that," "Don't even try," or "Being creative won't make you any money." Many of us bought into this limiting statement. It shows up now in our lives as the "Yes, but" virus. We hear ourselves saying, "Yes, but I'm not an artist." "Yes, but I never went to design school." "Yes, but I can't draw."

Creativity does not care about what you can't do. Creativity is the power behind "Can do." And whatever you can do, therein lies your creative power. You don't need art supplies or permission from your parents to create a better life filled with more creative solutions for yourself and others.

List Your Creative Self helps you recognize that creativity is built into your system. It is your foot tapping, your heart beating, and your mind wondering. Creativity is boundless; it is a self-generating force fueled by your imagination that morphs your thoughts into reality. If you can see it you can do it. If you can hear it you can say it. *List Your Creative Self* invites you to get your creativity muscle pumping by paying attention to your daydreams, your unfulfilled pieces of "wish-I-coulds" and "hope-I-cans." How about . . .

List the subjects and hobbies you'd love to pursue and master, from playing a musical instrument to speaking a foreign language, if you only had the time.

- Playing a hot jazz piano
- Skiing down from mountaintops
- Famous artist with exhibitions all over the world
- Successful tropical plant grower
- Fluent in five major languages

Just filling in the blanks will release your creative juices. Feel and taste the wonderful and boundless self-generating force that is your birthright. Sound powerful? It is. Sound dangerous? Only if you resist. Creativity invites you—actually, demands you—to eat dessert first, take another shower, and hang paintings outside your windows.

HOW TO USE THIS BOOK

First, give yourself freedom and choice. Start anywhere. No rules. No proper order. Close your eyes and open to any page and start listing. Just remember, the more you list the more you will fall into a creative state. The more creative you feel, the more you will build strength and comfort in using this very powerful inner resource.

Start by letting a stream of answers and reactions flow. Jot down whatever comes to mind. Even if you are not sure—let it all out. By doing so, you will create a flow of old thoughts that will inspire your present thinking, which will in turn inspire new thoughts. For example,

List all the possible things that have happened when you actually did what you *really* wanted to do.

- Found myself living in Manhattan and meeting unique people
- Found myself on top of a great temple in Guatemala from what started as a walk
- Was taken in by a family while traveling through Portugal
- Enjoyed the spotlight of a giant art show just from a single crazy idea
- Turned a simple "what-if" idea into a huge financial success

We need to create because it is human nature to solve, invent, and make creative solutions. Creativity is our signature style. It makes life experiences directly our own. This book helps you feel great simply from seeing and reminding yourself how rich your life and imagination already are.

We create because we are spiritual and physical beings constantly striving to make our world conform to how we think and feel about things. Creativity is a powerful form of expression that connects us both to our insights and to a higher and deeper level of self-determination.

By cultivating our creativity, we bring clarity and passion to the act and art of living. Creativity is exciting, energizing, grounding, and timeless. When we create, time stops and space expands; it is then, in that place of thought and action, that we express our truest selves. Our creativity also manifests real material contributions that ultimately form the landscape of our life. Above all, we create because we are here to make things, solve problems, and maybe even leave something for others to learn from and to remember us by. So please, have fun and be the creative human you were always meant to be.

CHAPTER 1

*Y*OUR FAVORITE THINGS

$\mathcal{L}$ist the treasures, doodads, and objects you've collected that inspire you.

_____

_____

_____

_____

_____

_____

_____

_____

_____

_____

_____

_____

_____

_____

_____

_____

_____

List the activities you feel passionate about.

_____

_____

_____

_____

_____

_____

_____

_____

_____

_____

_____

_____

_____

_____

_____

_____

_____

_____

_____

$\mathcal{L}$ist who you thought you wanted to be when you grew up.

_____

_____

_____

_____

_____

_____

_____

_____

_____

_____

_____

_____

_____

_____

_____

_____

_____

_____

$\mathcal{L}$ist what you like to do when you "play."

_____

_____

_____

_____

_____

_____

_____

_____

_____

_____

_____

_____

_____

_____

_____

_____

_____

_____

*L*ist the places your imagination takes you when you let it go wild.

_____

_____

_____

_____

_____

_____

_____

_____

_____

_____

_____

_____

_____

_____

_____

_____

_____

$\mathcal{L}$ist your most extraordinary talents.

_____

_____

_____

_____

_____

_____

_____

_____

_____

_____

_____

_____

_____

_____

_____

_____

_____

List all the art you'd like to collect if you had endless funds.

_____

_____

_____

_____

_____

_____

_____

_____

_____

_____

_____

_____

_____

_____

_____

_____

_____

_____

_____

*L*ist the pleasurable things you do for yourself that help you get through the workweek.

_____

_____

_____

_____

_____

_____

_____

_____

_____

_____

_____

_____

_____

_____

_____

_____

_____

_____

_____

$\mathcal{L}$ist the elements of the perfect creative day.

_____

_____

_____

_____

_____

_____

_____

_____

_____

_____

_____

_____

_____

_____

_____

_____

_____

List the magical moments you've had that you will never forget.

_____

_____

_____

_____

_____

_____

_____

_____

_____

_____

_____

_____

_____

_____

_____

_____

_____

_____

List the things in life that always bring you joy.

_____

_____

_____

_____

_____

_____

_____

_____

_____

_____

_____

_____

_____

_____

_____

_____

$\mathcal{L}$ist the colors you enjoy living with.

_____

_____

_____

_____

_____

_____

_____

_____

_____

_____

_____

_____

_____

_____

_____

_____

_____

_____

$\mathcal{L}$ist the things you do, from prayer to planting flowers, that make you feel more connected to your deepest self.

_____

_____

_____

_____

_____

_____

_____

_____

_____

_____

_____

_____

_____

_____

_____

_____

_____

List the most creative adventures, trips, and excursions you've taken.

_____

_____

_____

_____

_____

_____

_____

_____

_____

_____

_____

_____

_____

_____

_____

_____

_____

_____

List what you like to do when you have "free time."

_____

_____

_____

_____

_____

_____

_____

_____

_____

_____

_____

_____

_____

_____

_____

_____

_____

$\mathcal{L}$ist the things you find most beautiful.

_____

_____

_____

_____

_____

_____

_____

_____

_____

_____

_____

_____

_____

_____

_____

_____

_____

_____

CHAPTER 2

*S*AYS
WHO?

$\mathcal{L}$ist what your parents felt and told you about creative types of people.

_____

_____

_____

_____

_____

_____

_____

_____

_____

_____

_____

_____

_____

_____

_____

_____

_____

_____

_____

$\mathcal{L}$ist all the excuses you make for why you are not creating.

_____

_____

_____

_____

_____

_____

_____

_____

_____

_____

_____

_____

_____

_____

_____

_____

_____

_____

_____

$\mathcal{L}$ist the people who convinced you that being creative was relegated to only a few, and not you.

_____

_____

_____

_____

_____

_____

_____

_____

_____

_____

_____

_____

_____

_____

_____

_____

_____

$\mathcal{L}$ist all the reasons you believe being more creative might jeopardize your life.

_____

_____

_____

_____

_____

_____

_____

_____

_____

_____

_____

_____

_____

_____

_____

_____

$\mathcal{L}$ist all the reasons why your logical mind believes being creative might be a waste of time.

_____

_____

_____

_____

_____

_____

_____

_____

_____

_____

_____

_____

_____

_____

_____

_____

_____

_____

_____

$\mathcal{L}$ist all the things in the world that seem to keep getting in the way of your creativity.

_____

_____

_____

_____

_____

_____

_____

_____

_____

_____

_____

_____

_____

_____

_____

_____

$\mathscr{L}$ist what you think you'll have to give up to be more creative.

_____

_____

_____

_____

_____

_____

_____

_____

_____

_____

_____

_____

_____

_____

_____

_____

List the demons, critics, and voices that get in the way of your creative urges.

_____

_____

_____

_____

_____

_____

_____

_____

_____

_____

_____

_____

_____

_____

_____

_____

_____

_____

$\mathcal{L}$ist your greatest fears about letting your creativity flow.

_____

_____

_____

_____

_____

_____

_____

_____

_____

_____

_____

_____

_____

_____

_____

_____

_____

_____

_____

$\mathcal{L}$ist the people who are the most critical of your creative efforts.

_____

_____

_____

_____

_____

_____

_____

_____

_____

_____

_____

_____

_____

_____

_____

_____

_____

_____

_____

_____

_____

$\mathcal{L}$ist the qualities that make something "real art."

_____

_____

_____

_____

_____

_____

_____

_____

_____

_____

_____

_____

_____

_____

_____

_____

_____

_____

_____

_____

$\mathcal{L}$ist the times you expressed yourself and felt ashamed or embarrassed or got in trouble.

_____

_____

_____

_____

_____

_____

_____

_____

_____

_____

_____

_____

_____

_____

_____

_____

_____

_____

CHAPTER 3

You've Got the Power

$\mathcal{L}$ist the ways you could be more spontaneous, or a lot less conforming.

_____

_____

_____

_____

_____

_____

_____

_____

_____

_____

_____

_____

_____

_____

_____

_____

$\mathcal{L}$ist the rewards you give yourself for having completed a project or task.

_____

_____

_____

_____

_____

_____

_____

_____

_____

_____

_____

_____

_____

_____

_____

_____

_____

List some of the things you'd like to do around your home, garden, or office to make life more beautiful, functional, and enjoyable.

_____

_____

_____

_____

_____

_____

_____

_____

_____

_____

_____

_____

_____

_____

_____

_____

_____

_____

List the feats you'd attempt, from skydiving to leading an orchestra, if you had the courage.

_____

_____

_____

_____

_____

_____

_____

_____

_____

_____

_____

_____

_____

_____

_____

_____

$\mathcal{L}$ist the stuff, from clay to paint, that you'd like to sink your teeth into.

_____

_____

_____

_____

_____

_____

_____

_____

_____

_____

_____

_____

_____

_____

_____

_____

_____

_____

$\mathcal{L}$ist all the ways you'd like to remodel and redecorate your home if money were no object.

_____

_____

_____

_____

_____

_____

_____

_____

_____

_____

_____

_____

_____

_____

_____

_____

_____

_____

_____

List the elements of the perfect creative environment, be it a studio, office, barn, or playpen.

_____

_____

_____

_____

_____

_____

_____

_____

_____

_____

_____

_____

_____

_____

_____

_____

_____

List the ways you could take more time to smell the roses and experience being alive.

_____

_____

_____

_____

_____

_____

_____

_____

_____

_____

_____

_____

_____

_____

_____

_____

_____

$\mathcal{L}$ist all the things you could be doing instead of reading the paper or watching television.

_____

_____

_____

_____

_____

_____

_____

_____

_____

_____

_____

_____

_____

_____

_____

_____

_____

_____

$\mathcal{L}$ist how you would like to change the menus of fast-food joints across the country.

_____

_____

_____

_____

_____

_____

_____

_____

_____

_____

_____

_____

_____

_____

_____

_____

_____

$\mathcal{L}$ist how you'd like to redesign cars if you had the power to do so.

_____

_____

_____

_____

_____

_____

_____

_____

_____

_____

_____

_____

_____

_____

_____

_____

_____

_____

$\mathcal{L}$ist all the things in your own life you'd like to change by using a more creative approach.

_____

_____

_____

_____

_____

_____

_____

_____

_____

_____

_____

_____

_____

_____

_____

_____

_____

_____

$\mathcal{L}$ist the fall lineup for your own TV shows if you could choose any subject matter.

_____

_____

_____

_____

_____

_____

_____

_____

_____

_____

_____

_____

_____

_____

_____

_____

_____

_____

CHAPTER 4

HEROES

List all the creative people with whom you'd like to trade places.

_____

_____

_____

_____

_____

_____

_____

_____

_____

_____

_____

_____

_____

_____

_____

List the poets, artists, and musicians who have truly inspired you.

_____

_____

_____

_____

_____

_____

_____

_____

_____

_____

_____

_____

_____

_____

_____

_____

_____

_____

_____

$\mathcal{L}$ist the people who have supported and encouraged your creativity throughout your life.

_____

_____

_____

_____

_____

_____

_____

_____

_____

_____

_____

_____

_____

_____

_____

_____

_____

_____

_____

List the heroic fictional characters in books or films you feel express their truest selves.

_____

_____

_____

_____

_____

_____

_____

_____

_____

_____

_____

_____

_____

_____

_____

_____

_____

_____

_____

_____

_____

$\mathcal{L}$ist the most extraordinary artworks you have experienced, from paintings to music to architecture to gardens.

_____

_____

_____

_____

_____

_____

_____

_____

_____

_____

_____

_____

_____

_____

_____

_____

_____

$\mathcal{L}$ist your current friends and associates who truly nurture the best in you.

_____

_____

_____

_____

_____

_____

_____

_____

_____

_____

_____

_____

_____

_____

_____

_____

_____

_____

_____

_____

$\mathcal{L}$ist all the creative people, including sports stars, politicians, and scientists, whom you admire.

_____

_____

_____

_____

_____

_____

_____

_____

_____

_____

_____

_____

_____

_____

_____

_____

$\mathcal{L}$ist all the movies you've seen that made you want to create something, anything.

_____

_____

_____

_____

_____

_____

_____

_____

_____

_____

_____

_____

_____

_____

_____

_____

_____

_____

List all the art you've seen that has caused you to say, "I could do that."

_____

_____

_____

_____

_____

_____

_____

_____

_____

_____

_____

_____

_____

_____

_____

_____

_____

_____

List the teachers, mentors, or coaches who brought out your best.

_____

_____

_____

_____

_____

_____

_____

_____

_____

_____

_____

_____

_____

_____

_____

_____

_____

_____

List the most memorable civilizations and their early creations that you appreciate and admire.

_____

_____

_____

_____

_____

_____

_____

_____

_____

_____

_____

_____

_____

_____

_____

_____

CHAPTER 5

THOSE "WHAT-IFS..."

List the subjects and hobbies you'd love to pursue and master, from playing a musical instrument to speaking a foreign language, if you only had the time.

_____

_____

_____

_____

_____

_____

_____

_____

_____

_____

_____

_____

_____

_____

_____

_____

$\mathcal{L}$ist the stuff, from paying bills to doing the laundry, that seems to get in the way of relaxing, goofing off, or creative time.

_____

_____

_____

_____

_____

_____

_____

_____

_____

_____

_____

_____

_____

_____

_____

_____

_____

_____

List all the things, from lessons to art supplies, you wished you'd had as a kid that would have encouraged you to be more creative.

_____

_____

_____

_____

_____

_____

_____

_____

_____

_____

_____

_____

_____

_____

_____

_____

List your great "if only I could" ideas, thoughts, or masterpieces you have kept to yourself.

_____

_____

_____

_____

_____

_____

_____

_____

_____

_____

_____

_____

_____

_____

_____

_____

_____

_____

$\mathcal{L}$ist all the gadgets or devices you've thought up but haven't actually developed yet.

_____

_____

_____

_____

_____

_____

_____

_____

_____

_____

_____

_____

_____

_____

_____

_____

_____

_____

*L*ist all the good things that might occur if you actually explore your creative urges.

_____

_____

_____

_____

_____

_____

_____

_____

_____

_____

_____

_____

_____

_____

_____

_____

_____

_____

List the things you know you can do now but just haven't given yourself permission to try.

_____

_____

_____

_____

_____

_____

_____

_____

_____

_____

_____

_____

_____

_____

_____

_____

$\mathcal{L}$ist all the cool things you've invented in
your daydreams.

_____

_____

_____

_____

_____

_____

_____

_____

_____

_____

_____

_____

_____

_____

_____

_____

_____

$\mathcal{L}$ist your many forgotten dreams, plans, and ideas you'd like to resurrect.

_____

_____

_____

_____

_____

_____

_____

_____

_____

_____

_____

_____

_____

_____

_____

_____

_____

_____

List how your life would change if you suddenly became a creative success story.

_____

_____

_____

_____

_____

_____

_____

_____

_____

_____

_____

_____

_____

_____

_____

_____

_____

_____

_____

$\mathcal{L}$ist the things you would create if you were given an unlimited amount of time and money to do so.

_____

_____

_____

_____

_____

_____

_____

_____

_____

_____

_____

_____

_____

_____

_____

_____

_____

CHAPTER 6

PRIDE
AND JOY

List the things you do in your life that consistently bring you great joy.

_____

_____

_____

_____

_____

_____

_____

_____

_____

_____

_____

_____

_____

_____

_____

_____

_____

List all the things you've actually made that you display in your home or have given to friends.

_____

_____

_____

_____

_____

_____

_____

_____

_____

_____

_____

_____

_____

_____

_____

_____

_____

$\mathcal{L}$ist all the problems you've successfully solved by coming up with creative solutions.

_____

_____

_____

_____

_____

_____

_____

_____

_____

_____

_____

_____

_____

_____

_____

_____

_____

_____

_____

$\mathcal{L}$ist how you've expressed your creativity in the way you care for your family, your friends, your business, your health.

_____

_____

_____

_____

_____

_____

_____

_____

_____

_____

_____

_____

_____

_____

_____

_____

_____

List all the times you've truly committed yourself to a cause, a person, or a project.

$\mathcal{L}$ist the things you made or did when you were a kid that you received praise for.

_____

_____

_____

_____

_____

_____

_____

_____

_____

_____

_____

_____

_____

_____

_____

_____

_____

_____

_____

_____

$\mathcal{L}$ist some of the most creative ways you've gotten out of embarrassing situations.

_____

_____

_____

_____

_____

_____

_____

_____

_____

_____

_____

_____

_____

_____

_____

_____

_____

_____

$\mathcal{L}$ist the do-it-yourself projects you've accomplished around your home that you are most proud of.

_____

_____

_____

_____

_____

_____

_____

_____

_____

_____

_____

_____

_____

_____

_____

_____

_____

$\mathcal{L}$ist the things you do, like doodling, cooking, or singing, that come easily and naturally and that you love doing.

_____

_____

_____

_____

_____

_____

_____

_____

_____

_____

_____

_____

_____

_____

_____

_____

_L_ist the kooky things you've done, such as dressing the dog, baking a music box cake, or wearing purple lipstick, that you are secretly proud of.

_____

_____

_____

_____

_____

_____

_____

_____

_____

_____

_____

_____

_____

_____

_____

_____

List the accomplishments from your childhood you take the most pride in.

_____

_____

_____

_____

_____

_____

_____

_____

_____

_____

_____

_____

_____

_____

_____

_____

_____

$\mathcal{L}$ist the places you would feel great having your work seen and displayed.

_____

_____

_____

_____

_____

_____

_____

_____

_____

_____

_____

_____

_____

_____

_____

_____

_____

_____

$\mathcal{T}$HE
LIGHTBULB!

*L*ist all the creative opportunities that are currently available to you.

_____

_____

_____

_____

_____

_____

_____

_____

_____

_____

_____

_____

_____

_____

_____

_____

List the ways your creativity shows up, whether it be an itch, an urge, or a passion— you name it.

_____

_____

_____

_____

_____

_____

_____

_____

_____

_____

_____

_____

_____

_____

_____

_____

_____

_____

*L*ist the melodies, lyrics, images, and ideas that float through your mind during the day and inspire you.

_____

_____

_____

_____

_____

_____

_____

_____

_____

_____

_____

_____

_____

_____

_____

_____

List the feelings, from apprehension to anxiety to excitement, that come over you when you begin creating something from scratch.

_____

_____

_____

_____

_____

_____

_____

_____

_____

_____

_____

_____

_____

_____

_____

_____

_____

_____

List the "mistakes" you've made that turned into something "good."

_____

_____

_____

_____

_____

_____

_____

_____

_____

_____

_____

_____

_____

_____

_____

_____

_____

*L*ist the most remarkable coincidences
you've ever experienced.

_____

_____

_____

_____

_____

_____

_____

_____

_____

_____

_____

_____

_____

_____

_____

_____

_____

_____

_____

_____

$\mathcal{L}$ist all the positive things that have happened when you actually did what you *really* wanted to do.

_____

_____

_____

_____

_____

_____

_____

_____

_____

_____

_____

_____

_____

_____

_____

_____

_____

List all the doors that have magically opened for you to make your life work.

_____

_____

_____

_____

_____

_____

_____

_____

_____

_____

_____

_____

_____

_____

_____

_____

_____

List the music that feeds your soul.

_____

_____

_____

_____

_____

_____

_____

_____

_____

_____

_____

_____

_____

_____

_____

_____

_____

_____

List the places you want to visit that could help your creative juices flow.

_____

_____

_____

_____

_____

_____

_____

_____

_____

_____

_____

_____

_____

_____

_____

_____

_____

List the ways you creatively solve everyday dilemmas and situations.

_____

_____

_____

_____

_____

_____

_____

_____

_____

_____

_____

_____

_____

_____

_____

_____

List the things people have told you about your talents and charms that make you feel good about yourself.

_____

_____

_____

_____

_____

_____

_____

_____

_____

_____

_____

_____

_____

_____

_____

_____

CHAPTER 8

BRAVE NEW WORLD

$\mathcal{L}$ist what you would like to leave as your creative legacy.

_____

_____

_____

_____

_____

_____

_____

_____

_____

_____

_____

_____

_____

_____

_____

_____

_____

_L_ist what you'd do differently if you had it to do over.

_____

_____

_____

_____

_____

_____

_____

_____

_____

_____

_____

_____

_____

_____

_____

_____

_____

_____

List all the changes you'd make to the planet if you had the power to do so.

_____

_____

_____

_____

_____

_____

_____

_____

_____

_____

_____

_____

_____

_____

_____

_____

_____

_____

$\mathcal{L}$ist all the careers or jobs you'd love to experience for a little while.

_____

_____

_____

_____

_____

_____

_____

_____

_____

_____

_____

_____

_____

_____

_____

_____

_____

_____

_____

_____

List your creative goals or purpose.

_____

_____

_____

_____

_____

_____

_____

_____

_____

_____

_____

_____

_____

_____

_____

_____

_____

_____

_____

_____

_____

List how you might design the movie theaters and shopping malls of the future.

_____

_____

_____

_____

_____

_____

_____

_____

_____

_____

_____

_____

_____

_____

_____

_____

_____

_____

_____

_____

*L*ist how you could rearrange your days, using creative solutions, to affect positive changes in your life.

_____

_____

_____

_____

_____

_____

_____

_____

_____

_____

_____

_____

_____

_____

_____

_____

_____

_____

$\mathcal{L}$ist the events you would love to create that would make your life much more rewarding.

_____

_____

_____

_____

_____

_____

_____

_____

_____

_____

_____

_____

_____

_____

_____

_____

_____

_____

*L*ist what you'd like to contribute to your community to make it a really great place to inhabit.

_____

_____

_____

_____

_____

_____

_____

_____

_____

_____

_____

_____

_____

_____

_____

_____

_____

_____

$\mathcal{L}$ist the ways in which you could affect others in your life by being more creative.

_____

_____

_____

_____

_____

_____

_____

_____

_____

_____

_____

_____

_____

_____

_____

List how you would reorganize Main Street of your town if you were given free rein to do so.

_____

_____

_____

_____

_____

_____

_____

_____

_____

_____

_____

_____

_____

_____

_____

_____

_____

$\mathcal{L}$ist how you'd like to change your appearance or physical ability if you could.

_____

_____

_____

_____

_____

_____

_____

_____

_____

_____

_____

_____

_____

_____

_____

_____

_____

_____

_____

List the ways the world would be improved if more people claimed their own creativity instead of settling for the way things are now.

_____

_____

_____

_____

_____

_____

_____

_____

_____

_____

_____

_____

_____

_____

_____

_____